The Edible Alphabet Book

The Edible Alphabet Book

Vicki Ragan

Limericks by Shepard Barbash

A Bulfinch Press Book

Little, Brown and Company

Boston · New York · Toronto · London

First Edition

Library of Congress Cataloging-in-Publication Data

Ragan, Vicki.
    The edible alphabet book / Vicki Ragan ; limericks by Shepard Barbash. — 1st ed.
        p.   cm.
    ISBN 0–8212–2208–2
    1. Alphabet rhymes.   2. Food—Poetry.   3. Limericks.   I. Barbash, Shepard.
II. Title.
PS3568.A4113E35   1995
811'.54—dc20   94–47008

Bulfinch Press is an imprint and trademark of Little, Brown and Company (Inc.)
Published simultaneously in Canada by Little, Brown & Company (Canada) Limited

Printed in Singapore

To the memory of my father,
Donald Ragan, the original "Nut in the Navy"

Contents

Aa Aa Aa Aa Aa Aa Aa Aa Aa Aa Aa Aa

Apple and Arrowheads

Sing, O sweet Muse, of God's apple,
'Gainst which He sent poor Eve to grapple.
Seduced by her charms,
Mighty Tell spent his arms
And the Mac and the worm found their chapel.

Aa Aa Aa Aa Aa Aa Aa Aa Aa Aa Aa Aa

Bb Bb Bb Bb Bb Bb Bb Bb Bb Bb Bb

Banana and Baseballs

Slick-fielding Smoky Barbana
Played Single-A ball for Savannah.
Though cut down in his prime,
Smoky's fate was sublime
In both pudding and baseball arcana.

Bb Bb Bb Bb Bb Bb Bb Bb Bb Bb Bb

Cc Cc Cc Cc Cc Cc Cc Cc Cc Cc Cc

Cucumber Cowboys

Two greenhorns out ropin' for steer
Were each gored at a point very dear.
"Learn ya well," squeaked the Pop
To his son, with a hop,
"A man's front counts for more than his rear."

Cc Cc Cc Cc Cc Cc Cc Cc Cc Cc Cc

Dd Dd Dd Dd Dd Dd Dd Dd Dd Dd Dd

Dates on a Diet

Deviled eggs, donuts and jams,
Marshmallow-smothered baked yams . . .
"What the heck," sighed Miss Kate.
"I don't want to lose weight.
Besides, what's a date with no hams?"

Dd Dd Dd Dd Dd Dd Dd Dd Dd Dd Dd

Ee Ee Ee Ee Ee Ee Ee Ee Ee Ee Ee Ee

Eggplants in Egypt

Cleopatra adored a good eggplant
And sang to it many a descant.
But beneath all her hype
Antony had one gripe:
"Who can tell which one's ripe? I know *I* can't!"

Ee Ee Ee Ee Ee Ee Ee Ee Ee Ee Ee Ee

Ff Ff Ff Ff Ff Ff Ff Ff Ff Ff Ff Ff Ff

Figs in Flight

'Tis indeed a miraculous sight
To behold these sweet fowl in mid-flight.
So graceful and fair,
So incredibly rare,
To eat one just wouldn't be right.

Ff Ff Ff Ff Ff Ff Ff Ff Ff Ff Ff Ff Ff

Gg Gg Gg Gg Gg Gg Gg Gg Gg Gg Gg

Garlic in a Guitar Group

Though his rhythms are flawlessly paced
And his lyrics are perfectly chaste,
Still, the great public thinks,
"This guy really stinks!"
(Sigh) There's just no accounting for taste.

Gg Gg Gg Gg Gg Gg Gg Gg Gg Gg Gg

Hh Hh Hh Hh Hh Hh Hh Hh Hh Hh Hh

Honeydew with a Hamburger and a Hot Dog

A thick-bellied honey named Sue,
Disdaining her usual brew,
Set out to explore
Like a good carnivore
And came back with a nice barbecue.

Hh Hh Hh Hh Hh Hh Hh Hh Hh Hh Hh

Ii Ii Ii Ii Ii Ii Ii Ii Ii Ii Ii Ii Ii Ii Ii Ii

Indian Corn Ironing

Quickly go the autumn leaves,
Drop and curl in colored weaves,
While stoic corn,
For housework born,
Takes her time and time deceives.

Ii Ii Ii Ii Ii Ii Ii Ii Ii Ii Ii Ii Ii Ii Ii Ii

Jj Jj Jj Jj Jj Jj Jj Jj Jj Jj Jj Jj Jj Jj

Jumping Jalapeños

"Hallelujah!" exclaimed the two Jacks.
"NAFTA passed! No more vegetable tax!
We believe in free trade,
And we just made the grade:
'Extra hot' will be stamped 'cross our backs."

Jj Jj Jj Jj Jj Jj Jj Jj Jj Jj Jj Jj Jj Jj

Kk Kk Kk Kk Kk Kk Kk Kk Kk Kk

Kiwis in the Kitchen

Furry critters in the kitchen
Makin' chitchat started itchin',
Then a twitchin'
And a pitchin'.
No one warned them wine's bewitchin'.

Kk Kk Kk Kk Kk Kk Kk Kk Kk Kk

Ll Ll Ll Ll Ll Ll Ll Ll Ll Ll Ll Ll Ll Ll

Lettuce Lovers

On a soft green bed he sought her love
With honeyed words and silken glove.
But she so pure
Was yet unsure
And bade them heed cool heads above.

Ll Ll Ll Ll Ll Ll Ll Ll Ll Ll Ll Ll Ll Ll

Mm Mm Mm Mm Mm Mm Mm Mm Mm

Miss Mango's Manners

So well bred, could she possibly falter?
Why, even her rivals exalt her!
Bad soup or burnt cake,
There's nothing can shake
Good etiquette's Rock of Gibraltar.

Mm Mm Mm Mm Mm Mm Mm Mm Mm

Nn Nn Nn Nn Nn Nn Nn Nn Nn Nn Nn

Nuts in the Navy

Oblivious to gale and shoal,
Fearing not the cannon's roll,
They'll take a shelling
Without rebelling
And rule the seas from Pole to Pole.

Nn Nn Nn Nn Nn Nn Nn Nn Nn Nn Nn

Oo Oo Oo Oo Oo Oo Oo Oo Oo Oo Oo

Onions in Orbit

"That's my ship!" cried our boy Eddie Ray.
"Can't Mom play with your toys—just today?"
"Oh, all right," Eddie said,
"But move Aldrin ahead.
You *know* I hate onions, OK?"

Oo Oo Oo Oo Oo Oo Oo Oo Oo Oo Oo

Pp Pp Pp Pp Pp Pp Pp Pp Pp Pp Pp

Papa's New Potato

With pride and joy we announce the birth
Of Pinky—sweetest tot on earth:
One inch, one ounce,
All starch and bounce,
Our tender, bite-sized ball of mirth.

Pp Pp Pp Pp Pp Pp Pp Pp Pp Pp Pp

Qq Qq Qq Qq Qq Qq Qq Qq Qq Qq Qq

Quince Quartet

The quintessential Quince Quartet
Has topped the charts with an eclectic set:
A tart rendition
Of "Superstition"
And Mozart's Great G Minuet.

Qq Qq Qq Qq Qq Qq Qq Qq Qq Qq Qq

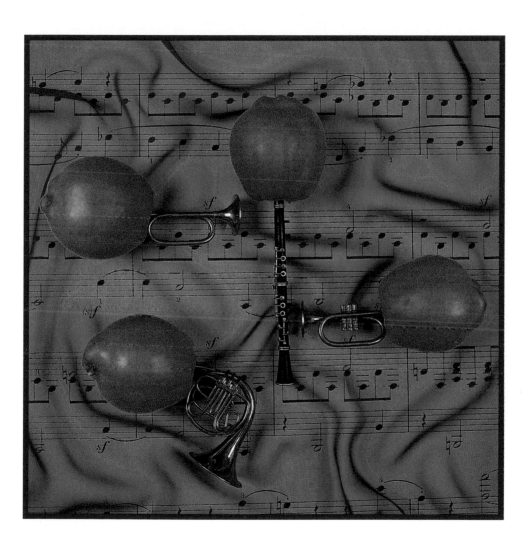

Rr Rr Rr Rr Rr Rr Rr Rr Rr Rr Rr Rr

Rabbit and Radishes

A bunny born into nobility,
Beseeching the gods of fertility,
Cried out for a son,
Then went home for some fun
And made heirs by the ton with agility.

Rr Rr Rr Rr Rr Rr Rr Rr Rr Rr Rr Rr

Ss Ss Ss Ss Ss Ss Ss Ss Ss Ss Ss Ss Ss

Scallions in Sneakers

A dashing Venetian rapscallion,
Persuading his mate to go dallyin',
Suggested they spoon
On a paprika dune.
"In broad daylight?" she laughed. "How Italian!"

Ss Ss Ss Ss Ss Ss Ss Ss Ss Ss Ss Ss Ss

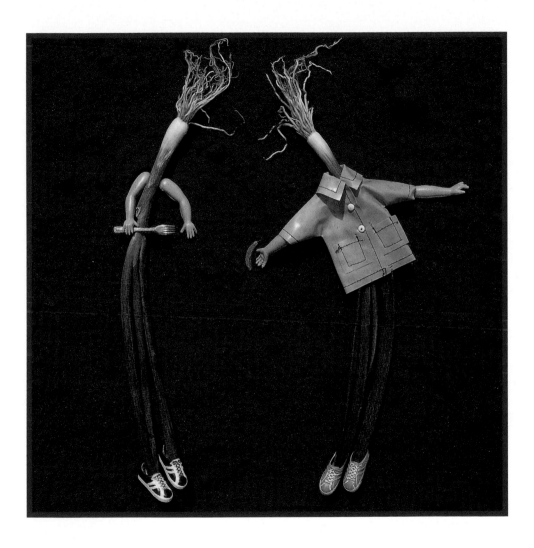

Tt Tt Tt Tt Tt Tt Tt Tt Tt Tt Tt Tt Tt

Tamarillo Talking on the Telephone

"What's this?" Tammy gasped. "That's incredible.
Such rumors are really regrettable.
I may not be sweet
Or so good raw to eat,
But how can they say I'm inedible?"

Tt Tt Tt Tt Tt Tt Tt Tt Tt Tt Tt Tt Tt

Uu Uu Uu Uu Uu Uu Uu Uu Uu Uu Uu

Uglifruit Under an Umbrella

A farmer grown bored with his fruit
Dared wander from Nature's good route.
To a grapefruit's fine genes
He attached tangerines',
Begetting this comely offshoot.

Uu Uu Uu Uu Uu Uu Uu Uu Uu Uu Uu

Vanilla Visiting a Volcano

Pity the poor vulcanologist.
Safer to be a seismologist.
For when *this* crater cracked,
It left only extract.
What drove them? Go ask a psychologist.

Ww Ww Ww Ww Ww Ww Ww Ww Ww

Wet Watermelon

Ms. Melon rolled down to the water,
Where lo! a great wave fairly caught her.
"No matter," said she.
"I've ballast for three,
And with fins I'm as quick as an otter."

Ww Ww Ww Ww Ww Ww Ww Ww Ww

Xx Xx Xx Xx Xx Xx Xx Xx Xx Xx Xx

eXtra Ugli

Call him ugly or call him exotic,
The effect of his face is hypnotic.
His looks are belied
By a mellow inside:
For a hybrid, he's not so neurotic.

Xx Xx Xx Xx Xx Xx Xx Xx Xx Xx Xx

Yy Yy Yy Yy Yy Yy Yy Yy Yy Yy Yy Yy

Yam with a Yo-Yo

A strapping young yahoo named Bo-Bo
Sad to say was a bit of a do-do.
He wielded his toy
With intent to destroy.
Said his mom: "Sonny boy, that's a no-no."

Yy Yy Yy Yy Yy Yy Yy Yy Yy Yy Yy Yy

Zz Zz Zz Zz Zz Zz Zz Zz Zz Zz Zz Zz Zz

Zucchinis with a Zebra

Real veggies have no use for limericks,
With their la-dee-da singsong and gimmericks.
But the zebra, my friend,
Stuck it out to the end
And (like you?) read not one but all twenty-six.

Zz Zz Zz Zz Zz Zz Zz Zz Zz Zz Zz Zz Zz

Acknowledgments

Many people had a hand in this book. Friends and family helped with the photographs. Thank you to Ann Simmons Myers for splashing watermelons and coloring Egyptians; Ed Bisese for sculpting volcanoes; and Susan Barbash for searching relentlessly to find the perfect fig.

I have been blessed as well with fine editors. Brian Hotchkiss had the brilliant idea to add limericks to the photos. Sarah Kirshner at Bulfinch was responsive, gracious, and wise.

Moral support came from all corners. A great big hug to my son, Eddie Ray, for putting up with the cannibalization of his toys, and to his cousins—Emma, Ani, Jonah, Lydia, and Sarah—for resisting the temptation to play with Aunt Vicki's toys. Thanks, Mikey, for cheering me on.

Finally, I want to thank my husband, Shepard, the Limerick King, for all his love and support, and for taking a break from his nonfiction world to come work for me.

Book design by Christopher Kuntze
Composed in Cooper Black and New Clarendon types
Printed and bound by Imago